Under The Pretence Of Love

A Debut Collection by
Zonara Haq

BookLeaf
Publishing

Presentation by *BookLeaf Publishing*

Web: www.bookleafpub.com

E-mail: info@bookleafpub.com

ISBN: 9789395088961

First edition 2023

ACKNOWLEDGEMENT

I would like to say thank you to my family who have supported me tirelessly through every journey I have ever embarked upon.

To my late parents; Rifat and Zulfiqar Ul-Haq. Without their love and support, none of this would have ever been possible.

To my wonderful late uncle; Irfan Bari who was a Pakistani novelist. Whom without, I would never have even picked up the pen to write. Your achievements helped me to believe in my dream.

And lastly, to the love who became my muse. You will forever remain a piece of my heart.

PREFACE

This collection is inspired by personal events and lifetime memories.

Rendezvous

That first touch.
My body knew this is what she had been waiting
for.
That kiss on my neck was ecstasy of the purest
kind.
It was all of my fantasies of you combined
together.

Hungry. Wild. Fervent. Hedonistic.

You were special; you always had been.

I had seen you sacrifice your desires for the
greater good..

But you caught me as I fell.
So I enveloped you and we pursued a lustful
love for the ages.

Rue

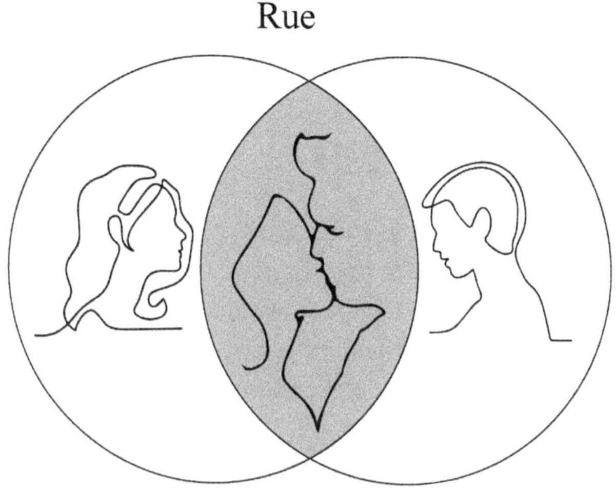

I rue the moments I never embraced you.
The moments I never told you how much you
meant to me.
The moments in which I'd seen your genius but
opted not to express my awe
The moments when I knew you would be the
greatest father but kept it to myself.
The moments when I held your head in my
hands, on my lap and silently contemplated how
blessed I was to have had a love like ours.

Warm Glow

I will leave the light on.

If you choose to come home.
If you choose to keep fighting.
If you choose to move forward and heal.
If you choose life over existence.
If you choose love over despair.

I will leave the light on.

The Banal

I was in it for life, the long run.
The slog.

The peaks and troughs.
The hardships which would prequel the ease.

I was there for the Love.

The snoring, the lack of sleeping space, the cold
feet.

The dinner followed by dessert.

What was your prerogative?

Love Of My Life

The inevitable has come.
Something I never wanted to think about.
Something I thought I would never need to
worry about.

The ultimate betrayal, we never knew existed.
The ultimate quake which destroyed the bond.

The waltz around the kitchen, the words, my
words:
"You are the love of my life!"
Echoing through the room.

I swear you could feel the love moving through
me, pouring out of my eyes as I gazed up at your
beautiful black locks and your wide almond
eyes. As you moved me around the kitchen and
brought me closer, accepting the warmth of my
embrace, the tenderness of my touch, the
softness of my kisses.

Those feelings, thoughts and touch seem all but
a world away.
Like something we lost. A far distant memory.

So was any of it real?
Was how you felt real?
How you touched me, held me close?
Everything you said, was it true?

Was any of our life together sincere?
Were any of our experiences together genuine?
Or am I simply wasting my memory of what I
lived through with you?

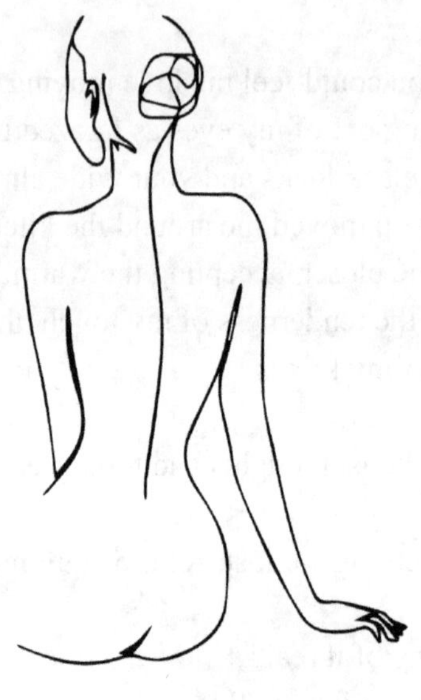

A Returned Gift

A woman was given.
A Love was given.
A heart was given.
An honour was given.
Broken promises were returned.

Flower Envy

You presented to me, like the flowers you
bought me.
Three months into our relationship, pretty to
look at, smelling mysterious.
An extensive amount of green with spots of
intriguing colours dotted through, I anticipated
what I would find as I dived further into the
bouquet.
You, yourself; were a sight to see, your beauty
cannot match that of so many men, even women.

Inside, I knew your heart was soft, but your
exterior was like that of the flowers, woody,
plain in
colour.
Your will as straggly and plain as the free
flowing leaves, where any small pressure of
force could tear them apart…
Butmuch like the flowers held together by
staples, you were held together by the glue of
your younger sister, your nephew.
Like a parasite in some ways, you grasped on to
signs of life which made you want to live, to feel
alive.

And even though you once told me, I was the
only thing that made you happy, the only thing
going well in your life. There came a day when I
didn't bring you as much joy as the colours of
the bouquet which you had gifted me.
I didn't bring you as much
sensuality as the smell of the lilies and so you
left.
You proceeded to rip me out of your life much
as those stubborn weeds looking for an
opportunity to thrive.
As if my existencewas not worth saving, worth
flourishing and nurturing.
As if I was not intricate and beautiful enough..

So I stopped admiring you, the excitement of the
initial flowering stages, although still there to
some extent for me, had passed for you and
when I realised what you had done.
I no longer see the flowers of value, but rather a
deception, whose price was far too high for their
worth and whose tepid colours had overcast the
beauty of the full bouquet.
And from my vase, I removed them
And put them in a place of much rest.
Just as I did with your beautiful, wishful
memory.

Mystery prevails

An unknown heart was loved.
When known.
It was broken.

Parasite

She gave and gave; abandoning her own wishes
and desires simply to please the creature she had
a hand in creating.

She nourished him from herself.
She cared for him in his self sabotage
and she relieved him in his self struggle.
She made all his flaws acceptable which
ultimately led to her own demise..

Until once again; the creature roamed free;
looking for the next selfless soul to consume.

Hindsight

A rolling tear
within each tear
a shattered future.

Self Sabotage

My heart aimlessly followed you into your
abyss.
My logic tried to haul me back but our affinity
was too powerful.

It lured me to you..

Hurting me but convincing me..
Reasoning with me; that the pain was worth it.

That this love was the real deal.

Natural Selection

Once Optimistic in reach of our goals, we
became enclosed in the finality that I hoped was
lifelong, something I had longed for.

But in a cruel twist of fate, as the days grew
within our union
Your love diminished; to that of the lowest of
levels.

"I have love for you.. But I don't love you."

Our once, fruitful and fulfilling relationship had
become lifeless.
We ran in routine yet out of touch, like friends
but strangers.

Our love had reached the depths of what was
possible. Our lives had touched one another and
our together experiences had taken us out of
symbiosis.

And as natural selection would have it:
A part of me died.

World of Our Own

Our blissful bubble.
Your enveloping embrace.
But, the outside calls.

The Strand

I left the last strand.

As a way to show you. I was still hanging on.
I still wanted you. I still thought we could grow
together.

But you severed it…
Without a shred of remorse.
But with much relief. As if I was your poison.
As if it was me, which had made you what you
had always been.

You severed the strand to forget.
The bubble in which we had lived.
The life which we had shared.
The story which we had begun.

Wish

Your wishful memory, a shooting star.
There for a promising moment.
But dead inside.

Lies

A wholehearted greeting he gave you, most
days; smiles and warmth.
Leaving his mask at the door. On occasion,
bringing it into your abode and storing it away.
In plain sight yet hidden.
As he had done with his alter self.
The glimpses of evil you would catch when he
thought you weren't looking. The flashes of
betrayal that your gut knew but your mind and
heart shrugged off. The face of reassurance and

love which was pasted together with the glue of
his habits. With the stickiness of his lies.

Save Me

I plead ignorance to your hedonistic nature.
I glorified a past life.
I took solace in "knowing" you had changed.
I took comfort in believing you wanted better.
I sacrificed myself to save you, till the bitter end.

Self-love

Love built us.
I nurtured you.
You comforted me.
Love convinced us.

Yet love of self broke us.

Pretence of Love

I was blinded by the pretence of love. That you
would never betray me. You would never reveal
my secrets.

I was blinded by your caring facade; that my
feelings meant something to you. That my pain
would cause you indescribable agony.

I was rendered sightless as I gazed into your
eyes which pierced my soul and hypnotised me
into becoming one with you..

And now I am scarred by the destruction you left
in your wake.
I am wounded with the knife you took to my
back.

I truly believed you would honour me; but your
inner demon convinced you otherwise.

My apology

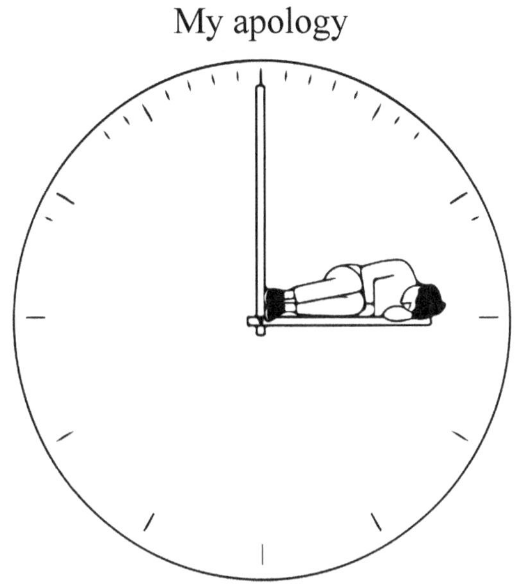

Amongst my emotional instability, my
irrationality and fear.
I lost sight of what was important..

What I had promised you. What I had vowed to
myself.
That I would always be there to protect you and
support you.
That I was your crutch so as long as you were
mine.

Somewhere between the tears and fighting, I
forgot to love you.

I betrayed your kindness, your gentleness and
your unconditional care.
And I will forever live with that regret.

Things I Left Unsaid

I laid my soul down, bared it to you. I only caught mere glimpses of yours.

I would speak and you listened. More closely than I would ever know, especially to the pauses, the unknown silences. You began to know me a lot better than I had ever known myself. My vulnerability gave you strength; all the while keeping me weak, as if my depletion rewarded you with accretion.
Yet you moved further and further away..

And I was angry.

That you may in fact have been my greatest gift, inspiration or possibly even curse. It frustrates me that my gut instinct didn't push me to react, to protect, to fight..

I was angry.

That my heart aimlessly decided to overrule my logic. Conclude it was better to enjoy the fleeting moments rather than plan for a future that was going to come.

That my heart chose to ignore the sense that I found wandered into my mind, time and time again..

But I am no longer angry.